TOLL ROAD
Somerset and Dorset Poems

Stephen Carroll was born in 1949 and brought up in London. He holds a first class degree in English and Creative Studies and has worked as a solicitor and law lecturer. He moved to Porlock on the West Somerset coast in 2006 and is married with three children. Twice shortlisted for the Wells Festival of Literature Poetry Prize, Stephen Carroll won the Wyvern Prize in 2014, and is the author of the novel *Venetian Cousins*, published by Andre Deutsch in 1995.

TOLL ROAD

Somerset and Dorset Poems

by

STEPHEN CARROLL

Illustrations by Nick Cotton

The Basket Press
Porlock

First published 2015 by The Basket Press,
Porlock, West Somerset, TA248PU

First Impression October 2015
Second Impression November 2015

ISBN-13: 978-1508899440

Acknowledgements

Some of these poems have appeared in The Starry Bough, the In Memoriam
Anthology and Midnight Skies, *Exmoor in Verse*.

For Henry and for Clive

CONTENTS

DORSET POEMS

INTRODUCTION

Looking at this selection of my poems it seems to me that my main subjects are landscape, myth and death.

As to the first, I have always found that to be outside is best and somehow the rhythms of walking and of thinking seem to suit each other. Walking is the best way of appreciating landscape; your viewpoint is constantly changing and you become part of the scene. Landscape in my part of the country includes meadows and orchards, high hills, cliffs, sea, salt marsh, woods and streams and of course sky and weather too. The enjoyment of being out in a landscape tells us that to be alive is a curious and wonderful phenomenon that should be appreciated while we have the chance. Landscape and my place in it is probably my main subject and I have tried to put the essence of my walks into these poems.

Closely related to landscape, is the spirit of place. How precious it is. Relentless urban and suburban expansion, increase in population, wealth and ease of access to the countryside all threaten it. Do we want to live in a country that is little more than an economic unit covered with anonymous dwellings and adjoining leisure areas? That is the future we will bequeath to future generations unless we become more sensitive to the spirit of place. Far too much has already been lost and once destroyed it can never be retrieved.

Linking the spirit of place to landscape, is myth. The landscape of the steep slopes of Exmoor with its woods, combes and streams where a person can be alone with nature can at times seem almost like the landscape of the classical world, and when sitting down by the rocky seashore or among the boulders and thorns up on the moor, under a blue sky, my thoughts have sometimes turned to the old myths and to the poets who wrote about them. Myths persist because they deal with matters that are the same now as they always were, things such as love, the mystery of being alive in this extraordinary world and the nature of death, something we become increasingly aware of as we grow older. And then there is the hunt, still so much a part of life on Exmoor. How ancient and primitive it is and how unreal it seems to a bystander. To hear the distant sound of the hunting horn and the baying of the hounds is to find oneself in a painting by Uccello or Titian.

I have chosen to divide the order of the poems in two according to county. The Somerset poems appear roughly in the order of the calendar year rather than in the order in which they were written. The Dorset poems all relate to the unexpected death of my brother at the end of October 2013.

As for the title, well, there are two toll roads in Porlock. The first runs for a little over four miles from the AA box at the top of Porlock Hill to the Ship Inn. The second begins near Ash Farm, where Coleridge is said to have written *Kubla Khan*, and passes the site of Ashley Combe, the house where Byron's daughter Ada Lovelace entertained the mathematician Babbage, to Porlock Weir and the sea. There is a third toll road which I have not as yet walked from end to end, which is not specific to Porlock. It is the one that exacts the heaviest toll of all. No-one comes back along that road.

Stephen Carroll, Porlock, October 2015

SOMERSET POEMS

1. THE MELANCHOLY OWL
(for Edward Thomas)

Beside the stream, the rain-wet road
that shines in moon and starlight O,
winds on to a place I've not yet trod,
the home of the melancholy owl, O.

I love the black buds on the ash
the margins by the river,
the song-thrush in the hawthorn hedge,
and the day that dies forever.

Over the distant hills I'm bound
by lane and copse and byway O,
for a silent land I've not yet found,
the home of the melancholy owl, O.

I see the brook now running free,
the mill beyond the meadow,
the magpie hanging from the tree
and the path that ends in shadow.

Will I leave behind what best I love
when the trees shake out their tresses O,
the message of the aspen grove
and the call of the melancholy owl, O?

2. BIRCHANGER

I sometimes sense his presence close behind
when walking in the woods alone.
We have our code, our way of doing things;
he always keeps his distance on the path
and knows I hear his footsteps echoing mine.
Sometimes, when heading down the track
I guess he's following me and turn around
to catch him out. He likes the game
and is too quick for me. He means no harm.
He's shyer than a girl and never speaks
and yet I know he's been there all the time.
Like me he loves the woods and waterfalls,
blackbird song, the raven and the jay.
He sees the line of footprints where I've been
after the snow perhaps or if my boots are wet.
He fits my prints exactly, leaves no trace
and understands my rituals and my quirks.
I worry about the future of my friend.
Will he look for me when I have gone,
wait at corners, fret like a little dog?

3.   WORTHY WOOD
Decuman, Beuno, Petrock, Dubricius

Footprints of pheasant, deer and fox
all neatly made in feathery snow
and lovely as the figures in a bestiary
now vanish from the margin of the page.
Into the dark they go, anonymous as monks,
their makers doomed to be devoured
by monsters, hunted by hallooing horsemen
or shot to the pervasive incense of cigars.
Such is the nature of life in the forest,
deep in the forest under a dark sun
in the twenty-first century of Our Lord.
Meanwhile the restless sea unfolds in the bleak bay,
bouncing off rocks like the heads of the saints.
Dead as ammonites, only their names live on.

4. JANUARY

Walking the high path, near the sea,
blue smoke drifts from far valley,
a mild morning, no sun seen,
but waterfall hides copper sheen
of rock-face stained with verdigris,
and fence that's red with bryony.
White gull, black crow, pink jay
all feast and forage in their way.
These common things all should
be written down in ink's black blood.

5.   A GAP IN THE CLOUDS

The elements have all changed places–
darkness and light, the sky and sea and land.
Footpaths have turned into streams.
Troughs and hollows are sealed with slabs
of hail welded together by frost. I hold one
to the light and feel my fingers burn.
The wind has lessened, but the blast
of last night's gale rhymes with the
morning's roaring sea. I watch from the high path
as it retreats and hurls itself against the bank,
retreats and comes again. And now
between the woods and waves, a jay swims
silently below me through the morning air.

6.   STILL WINTER

The hedge winds like a river down the hill,
there is no trace of colour in the sky
and yet the blackbird tries his song today
from the old oak at the wood's edge.
Out of the past he sings, or out of time to come
since now it is too soon for singing or for love
with snow on the hills and the puddles iced over.
But still he tries again so he'll be ready
for what he somehow knows must come
and I have heard of but I cannot see.

7. SAP

Blue smoke of bonfire
stings the eye, yet pleases,
as does the steam from
cowshed and stable yard.
Columns of incense hover in the frost.

A dog's bark echoes,
a distant chainsaw sings.
Lovely is the smell of sap
from a felled oak.
It is the smell of winter.

East Lynch

8. OUT OF THE BRAMBLE HEDGE

Out of the bramble hedge he came,
from the forest's edge. More wild than tame
he seemed, and troubled in his mind–
he'd have to be to sleep out in this wind
in these high woods, so far away from home.
He was a stranger. Where could he be from?
'Good morning,' I said, 'though cold it is today,'
but he said nothing as he went his way.
Out of the past he came, from a century ago,
I thought as I turned to watch him go
in tattered overcoat, his head bare,
his unkempt beard and straggling hair–
surely he was a man who once I knew?
And I stood amazed as the light grew.

9. CULBONE

i

As we step down into the snow
and silence and clear air, the lane
is two black stripes against the white,
and looking over fields of snow, we see
the coast of Wales a dozen miles away
beyond the ruffled silk of the sea.
Was it here that Palmer set his easel,
when he painted Culbone Church
or was it there, perhaps? Time changes
landscape, and perspectives shift.
It was less wooded then and now the trees
are thick and dark, hiding the way,
good cover for birds reared for the gun.

ii

Below us stands Ash Farm,
eight hundred feet above the sea
where some say Kubla Khan was written,
but then again, perhaps it was at
Broomstreet, or the Parsonage, that Coleridge
had his opium reverie; no-one
can say for certain where it was.
Where the lane ends a track turns down the hill,
stony, steep and littered with dead wood,
and a clear stream runs to the sea.
Somewhere near this spot, a boy,
following the hunt, stumbled upon the Master
sitting on the ground, and weeping for his pack.

The hounds had leapt into the air
after a stag, and flown into the void.
Myth would have fixed them in the sky as stars.

iii

Deep in the combe among the tangled trees,
beside a sturdy bridge, we spy a pair
of ancient cottages, and little Culbone Church.
Silent and humble, grey and snail-like,
it crouches by a holy stream,
where it has waited for a thousand years,
forgetting why, forgetting why...

The Lord will come and not be slow.
'He will return, he told us so!'

Ah yes, the coming of the Lord.
The moss is thick with frost on Culbone gate,
it furs the ferns and grasses on the bank.
Where lepers walked, a cat washes its paws.
This was a place for hermits and outcasts,
pilgrims, charcoal burners, mystics,
and, now, hikers with walking poles.

iv

The church is damp with no electric light,
and seats for only thirty-two. Hymn books
and prayer books wait inside the door
and the harmonium is covered with a rug;
it is indeed, a very English place.
Pevsner admired its setting and its shape,
mentioned the trees and rushing stream,

the Voysey lettering, but not the Norman font.
Sit here on what the worms have left
of this oak bench and you can feel
the many centuries of use.
Within these ancient walls,
the hunt and harvest were discussed,
births and deaths celebrated, victories announced,
and prayers were said for England's kings and queens.
Most of those who've worshipped here
are now lined up outside, under the earth,
their stories written in the land they farmed.

v
We sign the book and step outside again.
In that old gatehouse, Waistel Cooper lived,
a potter, now collectable, they say.
Hunched like a troll, he rode a B.S.A.
in shining Burne-Jones armour,
but then he upped and went away,
leaving his wife to prayer, sortilege,
and the harmonium:

And did those feet in ancient time
Walk upon England's mountains green?
And was the holy Lamb of God
In England's pleasant pastures seen?

She once saw Jesus in a dream,
but he, like Waistel, could not stay,
Now she lies over by the stream
and waits for Resurrection Day.

Bring me my bow of burning gold!
Bring me my arrows of desire...

vi

And so we find ourselves among the Culbone dead.
What can the stones tell us? That simple rhymes
were used, mistakes left standing,
that few, perhaps could read?
(One stone has two 'ands' writ together.)
Here are the farmers: Richards, Floyds and Reds;
the slow years took them from their lonely farms.
There are plenty of snowdrops round the graves
and plenty of bones beneath the flowers.

The day hangs like an unwound clock,
the long-boned corpses get no warmth,
the dog's bark echoes from the farm.
'Lie down and face Jerusalem!'

The harmonium is silent.
No one comes to pray.
The day of resurrection
seems very far away.

'Sing hallelujah for the Lord is come!'
'It is the hunt in down in the combe.
Lie down and face Jerusalem!'

Whoosh of wings, rattle and shake.
Now two more,
three, four...
chatter of bright jays plundering the yew,
flurry of jays where gravestones grew,
the tree of death, the tree of life,
Garrulus glandarius, chattering bird!

'Get up ye sluggards for the Lord is come!'
'He does not come, He will not come.
Lie down and face Jerusalem!'

vii
A mile on down the winding path through
woods of holly, yew and stunted oak,
we come to tunnels, steps and follies,
all that remains of Ashley Combe, a house,
where local youths, camping one summer night,
were woken by the gamekeeper, who said,
pointing his gun, I don't mind what you do
as long as you keep out of the pens.
(How those words echo in my mind).
The pens fence off Italian terraces
where Babbage talked with Byron's daughter
of algorithms and Difference Machines
and pondered on Don Juan gone to hell.

Where thinkers paced and struggled with ideas,
pheasants now hurl themselves against the wire.
Later the house became a children's home.
Rumours of horrors linger. The past is full of pain,
and the house, handsome in old photographs,
has vanished. Only the very old remember it.
Images soon fade. What was it really like,
this ghostly place in its sequestered dell?

viii
And, as we emerge from the dark wood
we see what visitors expect:
a gatehouse, thatched, with gothic windows,
a sloping meadow, and the little harbour
with its bobbing boats; a steel engraving
in a leather-bound collector's book.

The Culbone Cist

10.   JUPITER

As I looked out before bed last night
I couldn't help noticing
a bright but blurry light
in the eastern sky, quite low
just before you get to Orion.
I followed it with my eyes
as I turned back to the door.
Hypnotic it was,
like a slow-burning flame:
Jupiter with a million miles
to clock up before morning.

It was not something
for wise men to steer by
because an hour before dawn
when I looked from my window
it was hanging low in the west
having crossed from one side
of the universe to the other
in the space of a single night.

High above the familiar sea
the sentries in the Roman camp
leant on their spears, amazed
as somewhere over Fastnet or Lundy
Jupiter dropped slowly out of sight.

11.   AFTER THE SNOW

You'd never think that snow
would bring so many branches down:
pines and great oaks, limb and bough and tree,
leaving combes tangled and byways obstructed.
I was there when it began:
the day the sky was quite blanked out by snow
from dark to dark, and yet I walked my usual paths,
since weather is the realest thing we have.

Blessed by the snow, I carried on,
and made my way up to the very top,
where all was peaceful as an easy death,
silent and colourless and still.
Then in that solemn world of white,
the explosions started. Far and near
they went off, creak and crack and bang
with now and then a flurry of white dust

as branches shook themselves
and limbs fell to the ground,
or, with a crash, a tree that had withstood
so many storms, came down at last.
'A hurricane, perhaps?' a man said yesterday.
'The snow, only the snow,' I said,
and off he went, shaking his head in disbelief,
thinking me a madman of the woods.

Yet three weeks since the branches fell,
it's hard to believe the weight there is in snow,
though walking by the stream today,
I brush the tops of trees I never thought to climb,
and looking down the combe to Porlock Weir
I see thick bands of colour in the trees,
with orange tint on oak and burgundy of birch,
the wood's wounds something that the spring will heal.

12. WOODWIND

Wind changes the shape of sound
hollowing and rounding it,
fluting and oboeing the note,
and pruning the feeble efforts of the birds
with a saxophone grunt.
How that note slides up and down the scale.
Then there are the sudden booms
as if the world's about to end,
crashes of thunder, whistles and creaks.
This hairpin bend beneath the bank
is sheltered from the wind
which can't be felt; rest here and listen:
you can't tell sea from wind;
when streams crash down the rocks
they too can roar like oceans
or gales thrashing the tree-tops.

13. BOSSINGTON

The days before spring are days of waiting
for something half-expected to arrive.
Clouds race across windscreens,
Sunday walkers, still anchored to cars,
fidget and adjust their gear; dogs stretch
and yawn after wintering indoors.

The wind is sharp, bearing the bleats
of a hundred new-born lambs.
Nettle shoots look deceptively tender.
There is a trace of kindness in the air.
The oblique sunlight is somehow different:
colder, paler, waiting to come in.

Hawkcombe

14.   DEER CROSSING

It was a day of days: the clear air,
the shining pools in the marsh,
a thrush trying its song after winter,
and then, the gods being kind,
I saw, at the wood's edge,
a string of hinds begin to cross my path
with timid grace, aware of my eyes,
like girls after a ballet class
elegant in skin-tight leathers.
And strange to say, as in a myth,
my thoughts ran with them when they
skipped into the dusk, as if I'd changed
into something half human and half beast.
Sometimes, at night when clouds race
over the moon and the wind moans,
I think of them, out there,
watching, waiting...

15.   THE LONELY ROAD

From here I see as a buzzard sees;
the marsh, a thousand feet below, is a map,
and rain bursts on the hills like shot
dashed from the sky; the flesh wound cleft
in the dark wood, a mile away
is the new growth of larches,
and where the blackthorn curves out of sight
the bent hedge echoes the sea's foam.

Fragments of time, impossible to hold.
A mile on down the lonely road,
where the ash tree's purple flowers litter the bend,
I turn into a secret wood to find a hidden world
of primrose, violet and wood sorrel;
the thrush is suddenly silent, and after centuries
of wandering, knowing nothing of time,
the cuckoo calls. This moment I keep.

16.   BLACKBIRD

If I were asked to invent a religion
I would make the blackbird a god
and every day I'd go to a high place
and walk home slowly
through the broken light of the woods
with wisdom ringing in my ears.

And I when I got back to the world
I would listen to children and madmen
and learn how to avoid falling
through cracks in the pavement
so as to keep out of the pit
where blackbirds never sing.

Glenthorne

17. TODAY'S WEATHER

A day of sunshine, heavy showers,
blustery winds and primrose flowers,
fast-moving shadows, sharp-edged light,
curved lines of hedge a pleasing sight;
green fire of larch on steep hillside
where cliffs drop sheer to bleak seaside;
crescents of racing foam, black cloud,
and sudden gusts of wind so loud
that when all is suddenly still,
I hear the empty moment fill
with distant bleating and birdsong,
before it comes again, more strong;
and, when the hawk cuts through the day,
curving her wings as she banks away,
I turn for home, glad to have seen
some of what the day might mean.

18. SPRING DAY

Sweet as the sweetest shower of rain,
primrose and violets line the lane,
and shining leaves so small and raw
of bramble, nettle and sycamore.
Heaps of twigs and petals found,
by sudden gusts of wind blown down,
swept along in crescent line,
by bank of vetch and celandine.
The hawthorn's incense fills the air
the chaos of spring is everywhere,
and all the while the songbirds call
with blackbird lording over all,
till the hawk sweeps by with her scissor flight
on this day of windblown shade and light.

19. THE DIG

They stood against the skyline
like primitive tribesmen, and, for a moment,
I was half afraid, there in that lonely place,
but kept on, and when I reached the summit
saw them and others, grubby with work and mud
kneeling down like worshippers at prayer.
Each square was quartered like the wind:
here were the posts that held the roof,
there was the hearth, here flints were knapped,
and people lived their lives, such as they were.
The measure of those lives is sieved and charted,
the findings catalogued and packed away –
a broken pebble hammer and some shards
of flint – little to show, I thought,
for all those centuries of life.
I went on, and after half a mile
looked back to see the figures once again,
stark on the world's rim, watching me go.

20. SALIX

Diana, fastest runner in the school,
refused to marry any man who couldn't
beat her in a race; many tried and failed,
and hung their heads and died of shame.
When my turn came, I prayed all night
that when the pistol fired, I would be changed
into the swiftest hound. It worked,
and thus disguised, I overtook the girl,
bringing her down in the underwood.
I couldn't wait to claim my prize,
and licked her shining body with my tongue.
(How the spectators cheered.) Alas,
the field of victory was sown with salt;
for my impertinence, she stepped
into the stream and simply flowed away
like water. I am growing roots.
At night my branches will be hung with stars.

21. QUERCUS

In the heat of mid-day,
this landscape is Thessaly or Thrace,
the thorns and oaks classical in ancientness,
the lichened sunlit branches
grey limbs of olive trees,
the circling buzzard an eagle.

No nightingale sings, no boar appears,
the oak grove is silent. The day rests.

Below, a clear stream runs to the pool
where a figure waits for nymphs to gather
beside their jealous mistress, chaste Diana,
beautiful as the moon and every bit as cross.

She may come, yes, she may yet come!
Meanwhile the red-lipped satyr lurks,
amazed at his hairy legs.
Goddess of hunt and moon,
I hear your bold approach
with bow drawn hard against your breast
to fire the thrilling dart.

22.   SUBMARINE LANDSCAPE

Everything is luminous.
Oaks fumble for sky, their branches
the peculiar blue-green shade
of a cathedral roof.

Little darting fish sing
in cages of green coral
or flit to verdigris perches
in the velvet trees.

Under a green dome
long limbs of ash sway
like tendrils in the current.
These crisp dainties made

of copper-coloured lichen
have fallen into the air.
In a mirror-world
things reach downward for the light.

23. YARNER

These narrow lanes
embroidered with flowers
are lovelier than any girl:
a dog-rose tapestry,
of bramble and briar.

Forward or back
along the unravelled way?
Drugged air. Why should I fear
the foxglove's hieratic scrawl
indicating, to the chosen, honey?

There at the tunnel's end,
panting with dread
and expectation,
the helpless monster waits,
all too ignorant of myth.

Through a tangle of birdsong,
he raises his huge head,
and, unfurling a giant tongue,
stares with a sideways eye
which is both desperate and mad.

His bellowing is terrible.
How well I know him.
He is the minotaur,
forever trapped
in the long corridors of the night.

24. THE MOON

The moon's shadows are lovelier
than the sun's,
sharper yet more mysterious.

The moon specialises
in unexpected shapes
on grey backgrounds.

She invented modern art,
having an instinctive feel
for verticals and horizontals.

Best of all perhaps is her
work with follies, statues,
megaliths and stone circles,

her beech avenue series,
and the oblique lines and boxes
she paints on walls and doors.

She remains an enigmatic figure
refusing to give interviews
or to talk about her work.

25.   THE JAY

Descending the hill path that first time,
I dropped into the cackle and riot of rooks
circling below me in the oak wood.
When I'd got to it they'd gone,
with all their vulgar racketing,
leaving a place of silence, framed
by hurrying sky above and rushing stream below,
and a young jay dead on the ground
beside me, its downy breast
still warm, its body gorgeous
and unmarked save for a neat
gimlet hole behind the lolling head.
I pulled a dazzling feather from the wing
to keep (it fell out later on the train),
and went on down, leaving the body
to be stripped of glory like a god
dead on the field of battle at the close of day.

26. THE OLD ORCHARD

This marshy plot behind the broken wall,
beside the coast path, was an orchard once,
until the sea came in and murdered it;
but after twenty years, beneath the blackened trunks,
sea asters grow in thousands, and the autumn air
thrums with invading bees
all trampling the ragged purple stars,
which bend and sway beneath their weight
almost to the mud. Then up and away!
Honey and death. One day at a time.

27. HANGY DOWN

Smelling of cider in the sun,
the apples from the tree
are hollowed out by busy wasps,
the year drained empty,

For the paper heart of Shelley
plucked from the burning bars,
the singing time is over,
under the golden stars.

There's a sharp scent of death
under the apple tree.
For some there are no clocks,
or smell of melancholy.

28. EQUINOX

I watched you in the orchard.
You held an apple in your hand
and walked on slowly
looking down at the ground
as if in a mirror.

You were young and silent
and beautiful. You caught my eye
and glanced away,
it gave me hope. The air was warm
the leaves just turning

under a cloudless sky.
Then a chill wind got up
and I saw him sitting
in his sleek black limo
under the dark cypress

stroking his beard
impatiently.
He was waiting for you,
no ordinary man.
You wiped away a tear

and walked on silently
towards him,
getting into the car
like a dutiful daughter
brought to book.

The door closed quietly
and you were gone.
Only the smell of cigar smoke
lingered and an image of you
drifted in the air.

Pile's Mill

29. FALLING PLUMS

An orchard is a melancholy place,
how still it is. Where the only sound's
the random thud of plums, the mind
empties itself, surrenders to drowsiness.
Summer drowns in its own sweetness.

An orchard is a melancholy place
where wasps emerge from caves like tigers,
their shining bodies wet with blood—
how they struggle and crawl over each other!
Fury and ecstasy are one with the wasp,

a fallen plum is the flesh of a god.
Heaven is an orgy of sweetness.
It is time that drops from the bough.
The year dies with the fall of the plum.
An orchard is a melancholy place.

30. THE MIRROR

The toll road's surface makes a change from mud.
I like the vistas from the hairpin bends
through misty avenues of giant trees,
bends which turn five minutes of descent
into an hour of pleasant walking, steep,
yet not so steep you'd slip and break a leg,
though quiet enough for you to know the ewes
that watch in case you bring them food or death.

Familiar sensations: the scent
of pine-sap from the shattered tree,
the toll house generator starting up,
the wire dumped by the track, the roofless shed,
with all its slates lined up inside,
and sheets of rusty corrugated iron
which wail and whistle through the wood
when blown and rattled by the wind.

Traffic is light, there's sometimes none,
but on the day I am remembering,
down by the waterfall, I saw, sprawled on the tar,
a squirrel, killed by the van that passed, perhaps.
I stooped to look, and in the mirror of its eye,
I saw the road, bent trees,
and my distorted face stare back at me,
blue and transparent, like a ghost.

Not a significant event, I thought,
although it still comes back to me, that scene:
the bright blood and the empty vision
of myself, concerned and yet unreal.
Strange that on that day, as I walked home,
I did not know the subtle shift
this happening would make to my familiar world,
nor that another self would haunt me there.

Porlock Marsh

31. PORLOCK MARSH

'A breach in the shingle ridge caused by a storm in
1996 has not been repaired, and the bay has reverted
to salt marsh' *(from a sign erected by the National Trust)*.

Cross the plank bridge while you can,
it will be an island soon. This is the place
where creation and destruction
come and go with the tide,
where landscapes are made and unmade.
Here you can stand and watch
the pulse of water filling the marsh,
lapping onto mudflats,
creeping up deltas and silted tributaries,
insidious and inevitable as death.
Here the sea has murdered ranks of trees,
turned meadows into swamp
and the well-made barn into a gothic ruin.
Near it, they say, is a drowned forest
that swayed in the wind before
Pliocene and *Miocene* were written down.
Now, prints of heron and plover vanish
as bubbles rise from the mud,
and overhead the curlew calls,
knowing more about time than we think.

32. THE HUNT

The bus tipped me out in a sudden squall
blown from the west. My boots let in water
as I walked the wet track, but it was too late
to turn back. The farm in the distant valley
had all but disappeared behind
the smoking waves of rain, and when
the clouds shifted, the pools and ditches
in the marsh were suddenly filled with light.

I heard the buzzard mewing as it wheeled below,
and then a sound so far away,
that at first I strained to catch it,
lost in the combe, among waterfalls and wind.
It was the hunting horn, a good way off,
but nearer and yet nearer still, it came,
until the hullaballoo of yelping and bellowing
burst from some hidden track onto the road

inches away from where I stood:
the lolling tongues of loping hounds,
the thud of hooves, the scattered riders,
and the quad bikes in a cloud of diesel smoke.
Then, like the slamming of a book, they were gone,
and all was quiet save for the sound
my boots made as they echoed on the path
and for the heaving of the distant sea.

I walked on down, and through gigantic pines
I heard the horn sound from the combe,
like something from a hundred years ago.
It faded, and when the breathing of the sea
paused for a moment, all was still,
so that I seemed to drift far, far away,
and thought of other moments, other days,
and went on home and stepped back into time.

33.   OLD ROAD NEAR THE A39

Leaves of past autumns cover the old road.
The sound of traffic walls off a corridor
where brambles wave from the bank
and there are seasons instead of time.

Slabs of leaves now damp and dead
hide secrets that will not be read.
Faded by sun and washed with rain
their story won't be told again.
This stretch of old road is not long
a wicker cage of blackbird song.
The past, once clear for all to see,
has vanished quite to mystery.

Memory has its own roads,
and neither ghost of nightingale
nor wild rose wait for me today
where moths swam
in the headlamps. Instead,
a half-remembered smell of sour metal,
oil and leather hangs in the air,
and Father's voice above the engine note-
'Wake up, wake up, we're nearly there!'
There is more than one kind of ghost.

34. QUINCE

Polished and mellowed by the sun,
this quince glows
with childish innocence,
and yet its furrow and cleft
hint of forgotten sins
from long ago,
sins I would commit again
if I had the chance
and I remembered them.

Heavy and round it sits,
a fat year in a cupped palm:
starlight and sun,
soft rain and hail,
owl's call and blackbird song,
and sunshine that went on and on,
till October storms
ended the summer
and the leaves fell down.

And there it hung and shone
like a lantern all night long,
until a soft November day
when without a sound
I stole the last fruit from the tree.
And still it troubles me:
something in the scent of quince
older than incense,
familiar though as yet unfound.

35. MUSHROOMS

They stand like mourners round a grave,
bringing their own aura of stillness,
taking their turn in a landscape
into which they will dissolve.
They come and go in silence.
Many have skin that peels like desire
and smells of love,
others stink of the graveyard.
Angelic, gaudy, pure, disgusting,
they possess the keys to other worlds.
Older than ammonites,
stamped on by creatures long extinct,
they will be here long after we are gone.
They will not remember us.

36. BREAKER'S YARD

Near the Roman camp
where soldiers watched for invaders
is a dark wood
where nothing grows.

Your eyes adjust...

A dozen skeletons: skulls,
scapulae, rib-cages, femurs,
hanks of wool: junk.
This is the graveyard
where sheep are stripped
and dismantled like wrecked cars.

A puzzle...

Snow brings silence,
the world beyond the wood a blank.
This horned skull knows the answer.

37.   VALLEY OF BONES

This is the valley of bones,
where only death-calls are heard
above the winds and waters.
No man lives here
only the buzzard and the fox.

Passing the ribcage,
my landmark,
I hear the crowing cock
corralling his wives
in the faraway valley.

Listen! He thinks himself immortal...
Crow on old cock!

38.   THE COCKEREL

I used to hear him crowing
a mile off, celebrating,
and wished him well.
Then, heading home one day,
I met his owner tidying the plot.
in the faraway valley:

That fellow? He's a bully and no use
— may find himself left out for the fox.

The leaves have fallen since
my absent friend declared himself immortal.
That I miss his confident crow
would not console him,
nor that his widows huddle
in a corner like lost souls.

39.   ACTAEON AT PORLOCK WEIR

Down from the hills brave Actaeon flies,
His pack of hounds behind him,
With lolling tongues and doleful eyes,
They know that they must leave him.
His luck is dead, the day is dead,
And his hounds must grieve him;
Their tails are arcs of woe
A-hunting they will go.
Back you curs! O maladay!
Rocky, Samson, Hero, Demon!

Who is this so brazenly approaching ?
See bold Actaeon's daring leap;
Struck with love and fear he's gazing
At the water, cool and deep.
Diana's maidens shield her
From every trace of shame,
As Actaeon calls her name.
See the antlers on his head,
Actaeon is as good as dead!
Pachytos, Stricta, Lachne, Theron!

For spying on Diana at the Weir,
Actaeon has become a stag!
Amazement quickly turns to fear
As he leaps from crag to crag:
The hunter has become the quarry!
Winged, he turns his noble head,
Too late for Actaeon to be sorry.
Down, you curs, O maladay!
Sad the horn sounds, far away.
Melampus, Dromas, Napa, Haemon!

40. ROOK AND BUZZARD

High in the air, above the marsh,
a rook peels off and heads straight
for the wheeling buzzard in the sky.
They twist and jive and jink a while,
the old game: life, death. Hard to believe
a small mistake would bring one down
where ghostly carcasses of crabs
and other flotsam lie amongst the fringe
of bladderwrack washed up
by the sea's last surge.
The unfleshed bone is just a flick away.
Darkness and light seem just about the same.

41. WELLS, 9th NOVEMBER

Slowly they fall, the leaves,
settling into intricate unlikely patterns
on road, pavement and park.
Mist dulls the edges
of parapet and cornice,
shop front and market hall,
smudges colours, softens angles,
smothers footsteps and voices,
slows the images of the people
drifting like falling leaves
over the cobbles of the shining street.

42. BERRY CASTLE

Lonely as a hawk
ignorant of solitude and weather,
screened by a bestiary of trees

it floats above the sloping sea
under a mass of tangled bracken
writhing in a net of wind.

Though the sentry is a horned sheep,
and the ramparts treed and broken,
the place still lives.

Here they made things of beauty
skinned bulls, feasted,
buried their dead,

prayed to the old gods,
marvelled, perished
and fell into the pit

where time and dead leaves fall
and the old gods wait.
I feel them tugging at my coat.

43.   BLUE ANCHOR

Out there in a vast unceasing roar
the washed moon runs back
and forth along the glass:
Shannon, Rockall, Fastnet, Lundy.

A star bends, the windows shake,
a distant car light fades and the sea
slopes horribly. It is all wrong,
the land is drifting away.

Those black trees we've picnicked under
are in a frenzy, their thunderclap snappings
lost in the night. I try to sleep, imagining
the holiness of being out there.

Morning's pellucid light. Such stillness.
So this is what it's like to be dead:
a tree swaying all night in the wind
resting at last when the wind dies.

44.   HAILSTORM

Wind picks its subject like a lover.
In a gale one tree will start to throb and sway
while others standing by don't move at all.
This morning when the hailstorm came
I sheltered in the hollow by the pines.
At first the hailstones came in waves,
crescents of ice that broke and bounced
along the tar. But then the wind got up
and roared so loud my exclamations
and my murmured prayers were lost
as pellets driven by the sudden blast
swept down the road below me in a flood.
And I was grateful for the pines
that took the wind, awaiting their turn,
for trees will dance before they fall.

45.   ALL SOULS

Here in this bleak valley where only a pale sun shines
and nothing grows but lichen, moss and fern beneath the
   stunted oaks,
where time leaves no mark on the rocks in the hurrying
   stream,
and pigeons start out of the trees like the souls of the dead,
will they end their silence at last, the ones I have lost?
In a wilderness where sheep walk into the wood to die,
and clouds race over the sky and shut out the fading light,
will their spirits circle above like ravens after their prey
and murmur to me of the days we knew when their bones
   wore flesh
and their blood ran warm as we feasted before the fire?
No, that sound is only the roar of the stream hurrying to
   the ocean
as the cold wind howls and leaves lie rotting in heaps.

46. BENEDICITE

Looking towards Wales
on this ordinary day,
I saw where snow ended and field began
and white strips inside the hedges,
as below me, buzzards mewed and wheeled.

Looking towards Wales
on this ordinary day,
I saw rain, thick as smoke,
sweeping down the valley, and trees
dancing like green girls.

Looking towards Wales
on this ordinary day,
I saw a sheet of pearl reflecting soft
colours under a clear sky
and a sailing boat painted on glass.

Looking towards Wales
on this ordinary day,
I saw a shattered column of rainbow
under a Turner sky, losing itself in clouds,
appear and vanish again.

May I be granted more such
ordinary days, O Lord,
some lightning, and the songs of
Ananias, Azarias and Misael,
if it should please thee, O Lord.

47.   CHRISTMAS MORNING

Driving to church, that sharp bend
three seconds – four perhaps –
the loping body arched
in a final frozen leap
– a fox, only a fox –
a paper chain
of guts and tongue
on the tar, the red fur
brighter than the frosty air
the grinning jaw and glowing tail
a dowager's wrap, a brooch, a totem.

DORSET POEMS

48.   BOOKING THE CRUISE

This will be your final trip, Sir,
a long one, on the *Nox Perpetua?*
Your cabin's not yet ready,
but we don't get no complaints.

Here are the blueprints.
You'll have the one shown there?
I'll mark it down for you.
It has no window but it's snug enough

and there's a spacious deck up top
for those who need it. Here's
to a smooth unending journey
tracking the wheeling stars!

49. CHARON

Have your fare ready my friend.
I am the ferryman;
in time you will need me.
I am known by my cloak and beard,
not for my conversation
as you will appreciate,
though briefly.
I will take you to the dark shore
where you will forget
your woes, your blessings.
Forgiveness is not offered,
only oblivion.

50. AFTERWARDS

It was a warm November day
we gathered there beside the bier
and wheeled you over to the grave
where midges danced around at play.

We lowered you into a pit
dug from the side of Toller Down
well hidden from the light of day
since now you have no need of it.

Some words were said and we were gone
back to the inn at Wynyard's Gap
while you stayed there in Dorset earth
from where you will not come again.

51. THE HARVEST MOON
(after seeing the Palmers in the Ashmolean)

Beside the chiselled stooks of corn
the reapers bend in happy toil
between the folly and the scythe
under the crescent of the moon.

All the way back from Oxfordshire
we shared their immortality,
we hardly saw the day's decline,
the shadows over Gloucestershire.

No flaming comet, late or soon,
had burnt a warning in the sky
yet soon you walked your evening round
counting the quarters of the moon

unsure if it would come again;
then stepped into a lonely vault
hacked from a field on Toller Down
where all the stars process in vain

as do the phases of the moon.
How silent is that other world,
how long the slippered corridors
where flesh parts from the hidden bone.

52.   AT HIGHER GROUND

We buried him beside a hedge of coppiced ash
at the burial ground. To find it,
you take the Maiden Newton road
and turn left for Corsham. When you leave
the gravel of the car park, you start to
look around for clues. Nothing at first,
and then, after a while, you begin
to notice a pattern of bumps emerging,
a grid of grassy mounds,
like bronze age tumuli, dotting the field.

This is the heart of Hardy Country,
and the graves all face the view,
though why, none witteth,
since the unreligious dead
will never see the homely Wessex vale
and heights beloved of the old man.

Close by, on the A356,
invisible because of the hill's bulk,
a flock of giant masts crane
their long necks towards the stars.
They lean into the heavens
in all weathers and seasons
probing for age-old secrets.
Work on their demolition
has already begun.

53. LAMENT

There is no moon for him
or turning stars;
not for him the nightingale
or the old wars.

Sunlight does not know him
when the day begins;
nor are there any joys
or sins.

Beauty is not for him
or pain;
the light will not see him
ever again.

Time is not needed now
his sun has set;
let earth remember
what we forget.

54.   THE JOURNEY

'I dropped a penny in the
grave, to pay the ferryman,
an old one like the ones
we found in Mother's purse.

Have you got there yet?
Did Charon come to take you
to the place where, one day,
we shall meet again?

The first stage is not long,
they say, the only sound's
the lapping of a single oar
in the still water.

And did he leave you
on the wide beach
by the gate of Ocean
where the spirits loiter

under the dark trees?
I've heard the gibbering
of bats among the leaves
is the shades of the dead

as they converse,
longing for news of the upper air
for gossip, for scandal,
and the sun's sweet light.

Can you hear me brother?
Or have you found oblivion
in the region of perpetual gloom
under the black poplars?'

55.   AT A GRAVE NEAR EVERSHOT

Here lies one who had his turn
and now what's left rots here
beneath this grassy mound.

Pointless to doubt
the absolute nature of death
when his name and dates

swim here before my eyes.
Death is supposed to
nail things down

for good, but he
seems to be moving
steadily away from me,

like a comet
hurrying through space,
forever getting more remote.

56.   AT THE GRAVESIDE

A wet day, but still I went–
a month since he died.
By chance, there was another
at the graveside.

Wind blew from northward
with a whistling sound,
and sharp rain battered
the green mound.

'How are you and yours?'
the other said,
and we chatted lightly
above the dead.

There was no salt taste
in the cold rain,
which blurs grief
and smudges pain.

And soon together,
we turned to go,
our world being above ground,
his, below.

Sisters' Fountain

57.   THE ROAD HOME

On the way back from Weymouth
I looked through the glass at Maiden Castle,
and saw its ramparts black against the sunset,
with Venus overhead, bright in the twilight.

It was a cold night with the promise of frost.
On we drove, hoovering up white lines
in the sudden dark, heading for home.
Walls, trees and bends caught the headlights

and vanished again, and rows of cat's eyes
came and went, but Venus was constant
and stayed with us over my left shoulder,
clipping Frampton tower, skimming chimneys

at Maiden Newton and sliding through
the giant masts of Rampisham
where I began to look out for the graveyard.
I wanted to wave or say something as we passed

but went by as if nothing had happened
because the others knew and were watching,
wondering if I was all right,
and it was pointless anyway, you being dead

and not knowing. So I made no sign
and sped on, leaving you there
now part of the landscape, each of us moving
at his own slow pace under Venus.

A Wessex churchyard

58. BECOMING A LANDSCAPE

Was it only a year ago you walked
out of the shining pastoral
of inswept hills and chiselled wheat
into a cellar hacked from a Wessex field?
No wine matures in that dark place,
where time no longer happens
except to measure your decay.
How lonely is the kingdom of the dead,
how long the dormitories
where flesh blets on ripening bones.

Golden are the sheaves at the Ashmolean
where reapers bend in happy toil
beneath the folly and curved scythe;
for them the hawk forbears to swoop.
September came and no-one saw
the shadows cross the X-rayed fields.
Now you have entered a landscape
which in time you will become,
while the lonely self draws steadily away
forever getting more remote.

59. AFTER A YEAR

At the time I thought
if I make for that tree
when I come again
I'll find him. So I know

he's in there somewhere
by the field's edge,
near the ash tree fixed
in my head as a landmark.

But the place is somehow
wider than I remembered,
hazed as I was by the event.
Hard to think straight

when you're burying your brother.
I helped to wheel him over
on a bier. That bit was easier
than expected. Then we

lowered him into the grave
on ropes and stood around,
his widow hugged me bravely
and off we trooped

for refreshments after.
That was a year ago.
Here lies my brother
under a grassy blanket

sprinkled with dead leaves,
the brass plate stating
his name and dates
already looking worn.

We hadn't met for years
after the row, but he hinted
that he wanted me to
interrupt his solitude

if I happened to be passing.
I'm going to be buried
here myself
when the time comes

so we can carry on
our long silence
under the same stars.
I think he'd be amused by that.

The Basket Press
Porlock

Printed in Great Britain
by Amazon.co.uk, Ltd.,
Marston Gate.